JOHN PAUL II

JOHN PAUL II

PATRICK EDWARDS

BISON GROUP

First published in 1995 by
Bison Books Ltd
Kimbolton House
117A Fulham Road
London SW3 6RL

ISBN 1-85841-192-0

Printed in Spain

PAGE 1: *John Paul II in reflective mood in Glasgow during his 1982 tour of Britain.*

PAGES 2-3: *On his first visit to his native Poland as pope, Karol Wojtyla blesses his fellow countrymen.*

THESE PAGES: *The pope has a warm smile for 40,000 Swiss Catholics at an open-air mass in Lucerne.*

CONTENTS

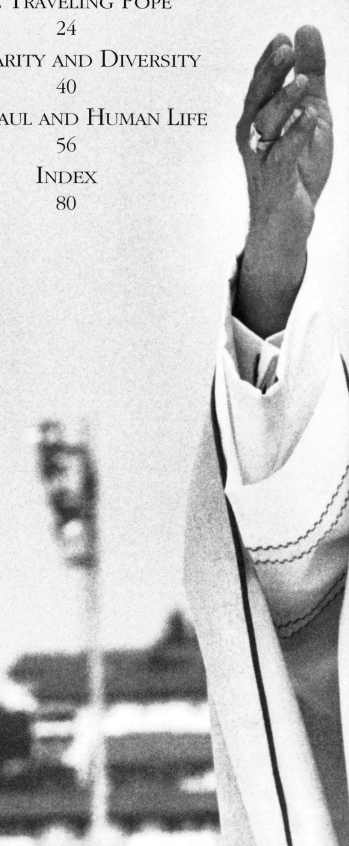

THE
EARLY YEARS

ABOVE: *By the time the war had ended Karol Wojtyla was a canon and was on his way to becoming a priest. He is pictured here in 1945, aged 25.*

RIGHT: *Emilia Wojtyla, Karol's devoted mother, with her little "Lolek," as she called him. She died tragically early when Karol was only nine years old.*

FAR RIGHT: *The historic Wawel Cathedral, the seat of the archbishop of Kracow, stands proudly on Wawel Hill overlooking Kracow. This beautiful city was to dominate Wojtyla's early life.*

Few could deny that Pope John Paul II has led a most remarkable life. By the age of 26, when he became a priest, Karol Wojtyla had suffered tragedies and endured hardships like no other pope in recent times. His father, mother, and only brother were all dead, and Wojtyla himself had come close to death twice in near fatal accidents. His homeland, which he loves dearly, had been invaded and its people subjected to unspeakable barbarity, and he had been forced into hiding after his religious and political views had made him a possible target of Nazi victimization. Yet from these harsh and austere beginnings emerged a man of deep humanity and unyielding love. When Karol Wojtyla became Pope John Paul II on October 16, 1978, the first Pole ever to hold the position, he brought with him a profound respect for human life and its capabilities that can only be understood in the light of his early acquaintance with human brutality and degradation.

This amazing story of endurance and faith began in a humble three-room apartment in the small Polish town of Wadowice, about 30 miles south-west of Kracow, where he was born on May 18, 1920. His father, also named Karol, had been a lieutenant in the Austro-Hungarian Army before becoming an official on the local draft board of the new Polish Army. Wojtyla's mother, Emilia, had been a school teacher before World War I, but was now forced to take in sewing to supplement her husband's meager salary. Karol also had a brother, Edmund, who was 14 years his elder.

The family apartment at 7 Koscielna Street was right next to the 650-year-old parish church of the Holy Virgin Mary, and it is fitting that the future pope should be baptized, receive his first holy communion, and be confirmed here, for throughout his life John Paul II has had a particular devotion to Mary. This was not unusual in Poland at this time, but one cannot help connecting this extraordinary devotion to "our most holy Mother" with the tragic death of his own mother shortly before Karol's ninth birthday. Always a some-

what frail woman, it is perhaps not surprising that she died giving birth to a stillborn girl at the age of 49.

This must have been an awful shock for her "Lolek," as she called him. For while his father loved him dearly, Karol senior "was very stern," as one friend recalled, whereas Emilia doted upon the boy to the point of spoiling him. There is a school picture of Karol taken the year after his mother's death, in which, pale and shaven bald, a face of almost eerie intensity stares at the camera with incredible wisdom and nobility. In a well-known recollection of their friend and neighbor Helena Szczepanska, Karol's mother would boast, "You wait, my Lolek will be a great man one day," and when you see the bearing of the young Wojtyla, it is not difficult to see why she thought this.

Karol's early life was not all gloom, however. Although he was known as a sensible and reserved boy, little prone to revealing his emotions, he was lively and well liked at school. A brilliant pupil

from an early age, Karol rarely received any marks lower than very good, as the numerous "*Bardzo dobry*" (very good) in his last school report show. Karol attended the local state primary school rather than a private religious school, as his father, despite his own strong faith, did not want him to be pushed into a seminary. According to his teacher and early mentor, Father Zacher, Karol "was the nearest thing to a genius [he] ever had the good fortune to teach."

Karol was also a keen sportsman, playing in goal for the school soccer team and reportedly agonizing over every goal that went in. He loved the outdoor life, especially in the foothills and mountains of southern Poland. Skiing, walking, swimming, and canoeing were favorite pastimes, and he was rarely happier in his youth than when among the high peaks and friendly Goral folk of the Tatra Mountains. This majestic range of the Carpathians, which straddles the border of Poland and Czechoslovakia, has formed a

LEFT: *Karol poses with a candle for a picture after his first holy communion in his local church of St. Mary's in his home town of Wadowice.*

RIGHT: *The young Wojtyla (top left) with some schoolmates. The future pope was a very able student and played in goal for the school soccer team.*

BELOW RIGHT: *Karol Wojtyla had a passion for the outdoors, and the mountains especially, since his childhood. Here he is in 1953 in the Bieszczady mountains in southern Poland.*

BELOW FAR RIGHT: *Even when Wojtyla was a bishop, he loved to leave the city behind and head up into his beloved Tatra Mountains to go skiing.*

spiritual retreat for the pope since his childhood. It is easy to see why: the beautiful alpine scenery is certainly inspiring.

On the path from Zakopane to the top of Kasparovy Wierch, one of the highest mountains in the range, there is a simple log cabin. Immersed in a silence broken only by the sound of a distant waterfall, it now serves as a shrine to "Brat Albert" (Brother Albert), a well-loved religious hermit who lived there for many years. Wojtyla must have passed this cabin on many occasions and longed for the simplicity of Brat Albert's existence. But this was not the path that the young Wojtyla's life would take, for he was always destined to use his talents for the benefit of others.

Three years after the death of Emilia, another tragedy was to strike the Wojtylas when Karol's elder brother Edmund died after contracting scarlet fever. He had just qualified as a doctor and caught the disease from a patient in his hospital. Both Karols were devastated. Now they only had each other. A sign of the boy's early spiritual maturity is given by Helena Szczepanska, who recalls her attempts at comforting him after his brother's death. "That was the will of God" was the young boy's simple reply to her efforts.

After showing some skill as an actor before leaving school in 1938, Karol and his father moved to Kracow, where the 18 year old was to attend the ancient Jagiellonian University. Kracow is one of the most impressive and historic of all Europe's cities, and it is central to the religious and intellectual heritage of all Poles. For centuries Wawel Cathedral and Wawel Castle, situated on a bluff overlooking the Vistula River, were the religious and political centers of Poland. The adjacent town center, with its university and enormous medieval town square and Cloth Hall, is perhaps the finest surviving example of a late medieval/renaissance city anywhere in Europe. In this remarkable environment Wojtyla began his studies in Polish philology and philosophy.

While always a devout Catholic, at this stage in his life Wojtyla had no ambitions to become a priest. He be-

came heavily involved in Kracow's theatrical scene and was well known for his powerful and beautiful voice, often reading epic Polish poetry at public meetings. Not surprisingly, he had dreams of becoming a great actor, and this first year at the university must have been one of the happier times in his life. But it was not to last. On September 1, 1939, Hitler's panzer divisions rolled across the Polish frontier, and despite the gallant attempts of the Polish Army, Poland was overrun with alarming speed. On the 17th, the Soviets also invaded Poland, quickly swallowing up the eastern third of the country, and

ABOVE: *In September 1939 the Nazis occupied Kracow, along with the rest of Poland. This wartime photograph shows a huge Nazi flag being raised outside the Royal Castle on Wawel Hill.*

ABOVE RIGHT: *Part of the famous Jagiellonian University in Kracow, one of the oldest universities in Europe, where Wojtyla studied before and during the war. Other well-known alumni include the astronomer Copernicus and Dr. Faustus.*

effective opposition soon ceased. The combined air and ground power of Hitler's *blitzkrieg* had simply overwhelmed the technically inferior Poles.

As a Slavic race, the Poles were deemed inferior by the Nazis and many were immediately pressed into service as menial or industrial labor to support the German war effort. In 1940 Wojtyla was sent to work for the Solway Chemical company, first in their quarry outside Kracow, where he hewed stones, and then in the water purification plant of their chemical works. He was one of the lucky ones.

By this stage many of his former tutors from the university were in concentration camps, as the Nazis began to carry out their avowed policy of exterminating all Polish intelligentsia, nobility, and unco-operative clergy.

Worse still was the fate of Poland's Jews. Kracow had a thriving Jewish district in Kazimierz, where over 100,000 people lived. At the end of the war only a few hundred remained, most were part of the three million Polish Jews killed in concentration camps such as Auschwitz and Birkenau, which were just a few miles to the west of Kracow. The fate of these Jews has always hung heavily on the pope. Even today, the streets of Kazimierz are largely deserted and pervaded with a strange sense of emptiness. For anyone living in Kracow both before and after the war, the contrast must have been horrifyingly clear.

Wojtyla attempted to carry on with his studies, along with many other students who formed an "underground" Jagiellonian, an activity which would have resulted in arrest or deportation if discovered. He also helped form the famous Rhapsodic Theater in August 1941 with his friend and former drama teacher Mieczyslaw Kotlarczyk. This secret group of theatrical patriots, most of whom were friends of Wojtyla's since his Wadowice days, would meet in small groups to perform patriotic Polish plays, Shakespearean and Greek tragedies, and to recite patriotic verse such as Adam Mickiewicz's epic poem *Pan Tadeusz*. It is doubtful whether the future pope would have survived the war if he had been caught in any of these activities.

Wojtyla continued to write poetry and plays throughout the war, but more importantly, in 1941 Karol underwent a spiritual transformation. His faith had always been strong, but in March of that year his father died, leaving him without

ABOVE FAR LEFT: *The Solway water purification plant where the future pope was forced to work by the Germans during World War II. Wojtyla had to carry large buckets of chemicals attached to yokes, he also worked in a quarry for part of the war.*

LEFT: *Some of the Soviet troops that "liberated" Poland in 1945. Their anti-aircraft gun guards the skies over Wawel Cathedral.*

ABOVE: *Cardinal Prince Adam Stefan Sapieha was one of Wojtyla's early mentors. When the situation became dangerous for the young trainee priest, Sapieha even hid Wojtyla in his Episcopal palace in Kracow.*

any immediate family. This event seemed to deepen his belief. Within a few months he had suffered a fractured skull after being hit by a tram, and shortly afterward he narrowly avoided being crushed by a truck, sustaining permanent damage to his back and shoulder. In some way, the trauma of these incidents, combined with the horrors of the occupation, convinced him that he should become a priest, and in 1942 he switched from Polish philology to theology in the "underground" university.

At this point Karol joined a prayer group organized by the tailor Jan Tyranowski, who was to become an important spiritual mentor, encouraging an interest in the Spanish Carmelite mystic, St. John of the Cross. This change of direction by Wojtyla is perhaps not as surprising as it might seem, for his nationalism itself had a religious fervor,

and as in many oppressed countries, there was a strong identification between religion and patriotism. The young Wojtyla was increasingly taken under the wing of Cardinal Adam Sapieha. The aristocratic prelate of Kracow had met Wojtyla in 1938 and had expressed the hope to his teacher that he become a priest, only to be disappointed at the response that his ambition lay in the theater. But Sapieha had never forgotten Wojtyla, and when the Nazis stepped up their campaign of brutal subjugation in 1944, Sapieha told Karol to leave his job at the chemical plant and took him into hiding in the cardinal's palace.

This occurred just after Wojtyla had miraculously avoided arrest when troops failed to search his flat during an attempt to arrest all adult males in his Debniki district of Kracow. Wojtyla was by now also actively involved in distributing false papers to Jews to help them evade arrest and even distributed patriotic propaganda in the streets of Kracow in the last few months of the war.

Kracow was finally "liberated" by the Soviets in January 1945 and Wojtyla was set to work helping to clean up the seminary and the buildings of the university. Shortly after resuming his studies in theology, Karol Wojtyla was ordained on November 1, 1946 by his mentor and protector, Cardinal Sapieha. This remarkable young man had already experienced, by the age of 26, more of the trials and tragedy of human existence than most popes experience in a lifetime. Not only had he lived through the horrors of a world war and seen his country dismembered, he had also been witness to one of the most evil and calculated acts of genocide in human history and seen all his immediate family die. On November 15 the young priest left Poland for Rome to study at the Angelicum, thus beginning an odyssey which would take him back to Rome in a very different capacity 32 years later. But wherever he went, he carried the scars of these years which, perhaps more than any other period in his life, laid the foundations of his principles and beliefs.

FROM PRIEST TO POPE

LEFT: *When Cardinal Wojtyla was made the first non-Italian pope for 450 years by the cardinals on October 16, 1978, he was a relative unknown outside of his native Poland. But at least one Italian nun seems to know what he looks like.*

ABOVE: *The young deacon Wojtyla (center) with his fellow seminarians in 1946.*

RIGHT: *When Wojtyla became pope he never abandoned the dedication to pastoral care for which he was known as a young priest. Here he visits a hospital in Scotland in 1982.*

LEFT: *As a young priest at the large Kracow parish of St. Florian's, Wojtyla was extremely popular, but his mentor, Cardinal Sapieba, felt he was being smothered by his parishioners' affection and decided he should return to academia to study for a second doctorate.*

RIGHT: *Cardinal Basil Hume, in the red cassock and white stole, looks on as John Paul II addresses the congregation in London's Southwark Cathedral during his tour in 1982.*

BELOW: *John Paul II's old friend and former superior as Primate of Poland, Cardinal Stefan Wyszynski, poses next to the newly elected pontiff. Wyszynski was naturally delighted with the appointment.*

The young priest was immediately sent to Rome to continue his education and fill in the gaps that were the inevitable consequence of his underground studies. Taking up residence at the Belgian College, Father Wojtyla attended the Dominican-run Angelicum (later known as The Pontifical University of St. Thomas). His doctoral thesis on the Doctrine of Faith according to St. John of the Cross not only reflected his wartime spiritual influences, but plunged him into a theological controversy within the Church. His supervisor, Reginald Garrigou-Lagrange, was a leading defender of the traditional interpretation of St. Thomas Aquinas, the medieval philosopher whose thought underpins so much Catholic theology, but some theologians, such as Karl Rahner, were beginning to question the

Wojtyla then returned to Rome to finish his thesis, which was accepted *magna cum laude*, and the young Doctor of Divinity was soon back in his native Poland to take up his first parochial position.

The small village of Niegowic, 130 miles from Kracow, was the unlikely destination for the intellectual and well-traveled priest. After initial disquiet at the ascetic nature (and disheveled appearance) of their new priest, the villagers soon came to recognize his talents and virtues. After a few months they asked him for advice on how they should celebrate the 50th anniversary of their parish priest, his radical suggestion was to build a new church! The resulting building stands as a lasting monument to his inspirational powers to this day.

After eight months, Wojtyla returned to Kracow, to the large parish of St. Florian, but it was not an entirely happy homecoming. By 1949, the Polish Communist party, under the direction of the Soviets, was beginning to flex its muscles. All religion is anathema to orthodox Marxists, who believe that the sum total of human experience is to be found in the material world. Communists saw the Church as at best an irrelevance, and at worst a dangerous anti-revolutionary bourgeois element within the state. Marxists argued, and not without good reason, that by directing human goals away from this world and toward the next, Christianity had prevented the proletariat from seeking redress for their economic grievances and had acted as a bulwark of the capitalist system. Whatever the merits or demerits of this argument in general, it seriously misrepresented the function of the Catholic church in Poland. Here, the Church had become so closely associated with national aspirations in times of subjugation that it was usually seen as a liberating and unifying force rather than an oppressive and divisive one.

However, the Communist state embarked on a program of systematic attacks on the Church, which included closing or persecuting Catholic educational establishments, banning Catholic organizations, restricting their publica-

accepted interpretation of Thomist thought in a movement that became known as The New Theology. It is difficult to assess the influence of Garrigou-Lagrange on Wojtyla's later thinking but his traditional education would not have been out of place at the Angelicum.

Wojtyla was soon dealing with less esoteric matters, however, during a summer in France working with the innovative "Mission de France," which

was attempting to tackle the problem of declining adherence to Catholicism among the working classes by putting priests in the workplace. He became interested in the emerging Young Christian Workers movement, which was trying to provide some spiritual focus for an urban youth increasingly cut off from traditional values and society. He brought this interest in the problems of the young in a modern society back to Poland and has maintained it ever since.

tions, and imprisoning hundreds of priests. It was in this difficult atmosphere that Wojtyla began his ministry in Kracow. But the faith of many Poles was extremely strong, and the young priest's undoubted preaching abilities attracted huge congregations. His homilies on ethical matters were so well regarded that many students from the university attended, and Wojtyla's parishioners loved him dearly, especially the young ones, with whom he would play soccer and discuss the theater and film.

In 1951, just before he died, Wojtyla's patron, Cardinal Sapieha, decided that Wojtyla should be relieved of his pastoral duties to renew his theological and philosophical studies. Wojtyla's new superior, Archbishop Baziak, rejected Karol's appeal that he be allowed some pastoral function, despite his undoubted popularity in the parish. Wojtyla moved in with his former Jagiellonian professor, Father Rozycki, (who had originally suggested the idea of Wojtyla returning to academia to Sapieha) and began a second doctorate on the possibility of building a Christian ethic on the principles of the German philosopher Max Scheler. Two years later he began lecturing in clandestine on ethics and theology at the illegal seminary in Kracow, and his favorable reception led to a lectureship in ethics at the independently-funded Catholic University of Lublin. He enjoyed being around students again and they obviously enjoyed his teaching, for he was soon elevated to a professorship.

Wojtyla continued to teach in both Kracow and Lublin, pursuing a hectic schedule which involved commuting between the two cities (about 160 miles apart) by overnight train, and it was not long before his unusual combination of pastoral and intellectual abilities were recognized. In 1958 he became Poland's youngest bishop at the age of 38. He took as his motto the phrase "*Totus Tuus*" (totally yours), which aptly summarizes the humility and devotion to duty he has always exhibited.

This rapid rise had taken place against a backdrop of government persecution that had seen over 1000 Polish priests

imprisoned, including the Polish primate, Cardinal Wyszynski. The antagonism between Church and state was made worse by the papacy's refusal to recognize the former German territories given to Poland after the war by appointing bishops to their diocese. Cardinals Sapieha and Wyszynski, who like all Polish patriots felt as strongly about the matter as the Communist government, both failed in their attempts to persuade Pius XII to recognize these areas as Polish. The realization that Rome was unwilling to help with the difficult and potentially compromising process of dealing with a Communist state led the Polish church to conclude its own agreement with the Communists, which recognized the legitimacy of the state in return for a relaxation of the religious persecution.

For a time this eased the Church's struggle. However, the determination of Cardinal Wyszynski to initiate a 10-year preparation for the celebration of 1000 years of Polish Christianity in 1966 caused tension to rise once again as this date approached. The appeals to Mary,

the Queen of Poland, may have lacked a material threat to the state, but they were an obvious declaration that the present government was illegitimate in the eyes of many Catholic Poles.

During this period, in addition to his duties as priest and teacher, the new bishop Wojtyla published poetry such as *The Quarry*. This work, which reveals his deep respect for work as a fundamental human experience and was obviously based on his wartime experience, was published under the pseudonym Andrzej Jawien. Jawien stands for "revealer of truth."

As well as poetry, Wojtyla began writing religious works for publication. *Love and Responsibility*, written in 1960, is an early statement of his conservative attitudes toward sexuality and relationships. It is entirely concerned with monogamous, married relationships and although he has much to say about the necessity of giving oneself wholly to a partner, he sees their primary purpose as procreation in line with traditional teaching. He also expounds the view that artificial contra-

FAR LEFT ABOVE: *In 1967 Archbishop Wojtyla of Kracow was made a cardinal by Pope Paul VI. At the time he was thought by many to be a liberal after his contributions to Vatican II. Cardinal Wyszynski can be seen behind Wojtyla.*

FAR LEFT: *This photograph shows John Paul as Cardinal Wojtyla of Kracow shortly before his, at the time, surprising election to the papacy.*

ABOVE: *Pope John XXIII is carried aloft from the Vatican Palace to St. Peter's Basilica for the opening of the great ecumenical council (which later became known as Vatican II) in 1962. Tragically he died within a year but will always be remembered as the pope who forced the Catholic church to address the problems of twentieth-century life.*

ception is a violation of natural (and hence God-given) laws: his thinking on this issue has not altered significantly since.

By the time Wojtyla attended the Second Vatican Council in October 1962 (called by Pope John XXIII in 1959), he was administrator of the diocese of Kracow, following the death in June of his superior Archbishop Baziak. By the end of the following year he had become archbishop of Kracow and was rapidly making a name for himself on the committees of the historic council. Vatican II lasted until 1965, and by then Pope Paul VI had certainly recognized the abilities of the young archbishop from Poland. The influence of Wojtyla on Vatican II was important and complex. Despite recent criticism, his opinions are best characterized as neither wholly traditional nor wholly modern. For in addition to his conservative views on sexuality and marriage, he was also a strong advocate of religious liberty, and sought to enhance the standing and importance of the general laity in the eyes of his clerical colleagues.

In 1967 Poland had a second cardinal, but Wojtyla's new position did not prevent him from skiing and writing in addition to the punishing schedule he

ABOVE: *Cardinal Wojtyla meets Canadian Poles as he takes part in the 25th anniversary of the Polish Canadian Congress in Montreal in August 1969.*

RIGHT: *In their traditional dress, the Goral folk of the Tatra Mountains greet the future pope during his time as Cardinal Wojtyla of Kracow.*

ABOVE RIGHT: *The city of Chicago has a large Polish population. John Paul II poses here with its Polish Cardinal Krol in 1974 while still a cardinal himself.*

FAR RIGHT: *John Paul II preaches at an open-air mass in York, England, in May 1982.*

set himself in Kracow and at the synods of bishops set up by Vatican II. Wojtyla's participation in these synods, and in the congregations for liturgy and sacraments, Catholic education, and the clergy, continued to broaden his horizons. Before Vatican II it could be said that he was largely preoccupied with Polish Catholicism, but the council changed him, and he began to develop a genuine appreciation and knowledge of the worldwide Church. This was further enhanced by the beginning of what was to become a central feature of his papacy: the foreign tour.

In the period from 1969 to 1976, Cardinal Wojtyla made numerous trips to western Europe, North America, and Australia, and corresponded with many Third World bishops. John Paul II is also a great linguist, with knowledge of over 20 languages, including German, Italian,

French, English, Spanish, Russian, Ukrainian, Czech, as well as Latin, Greek, Hebrew, and, of course, Polish. By the time of his election to the papacy he had impressive international credentials as leader of a global Church. However, he has always maintained a particular love and concern for his countrymen, seeking out Polish communities during his visits abroad.

As a sign of his growing stature within the Church, in 1976 he was invited by Pope Paul VI to give the lectures for that year's Lenten retreat of the pope and members of the Curia. His theme was the mystery of the incarnation as symbolized by the image of the cross, wherein "lies the full truth about man, man's true stature, his wretchedness and his grandeur, his worth and the price paid for him." These meditations deeply impressed all present and were later published under the title *A Sign of Contradiction*.

As we already know, there is more to Karol Wojtyla than his spirituality and intellectual prowess: his strength and force of personality are also vital parts of his persona. These qualities were never better demonstrated than in his determination to build a church in the Stalinist model industrial town of Nowa Huta. The Communists placed many obstacles in the way of the project and at one stage refused permission outright, but after pitched battles in the streets of Nowa Huta in 1960 they relented and Cardinal Wojtyla began the building work himself in October 1967. A constant source of support to the volunteers who were constructing the church, he consecrated the church on May 17, 1977.

On August 6, 1978, Pope Paul VI died at the papal summer residence, Castel Gandolfo. Cardinal Wojtyla, along with all the other cardinals, was summoned to Rome to choose his successor. After the perceived distance and stagnation of the last years of Paul VI's papacy, the cardinals were looking for a more human, pastoral pope. They elected Cardinal Albino Luciani of Venice, who took the name John Paul I, but sadly the "smiling pope" died only 33 days after his election.

Inconsistent Vatican statements and undue secrecy gave rise to numerous conspiracy theories about his death, but the most plausible explanation is that he died of a heart attack brought on by the strain of the office. Despite his undoubted charm and appeal, Vatican insiders had begun to show concern about his suitability for such a physically and intellectually demanding position even before his death. The new pope would have to have extraordinary mental and physical vigor as well as remarkable powers of inspiration and communication.

Although Cardinal Wojtyla himself seemed to think he had little chance of being elected when he arrived in Rome for the second college of cardinals in two months (he had made plans to return to Poland straight after the elec-

tion), many were beginning to canvas the opinion that the time had come for a non-Italian pope. The early ballots did not immediately reflect this opinion as the college was fundamentally split between two Italians (the relatively liberal cardinal of Florence, Giovanni Benelli, and the conservative Cardinal Siri of Genoa), but neither of them could achieve the 75 votes needed.

Cardinal Wojtyla had received some early votes but it was only after the sixth or seventh ballot, when the cardinals were asked to reconsider their positions, that they began to transfer their allegiance to Cardinal Wojtyla. These proceedings are always shrouded in mystery, but it seems that on the eighth ballot Wojtyla received an impressive total of around 100 votes. The Catholic church had a new leader.

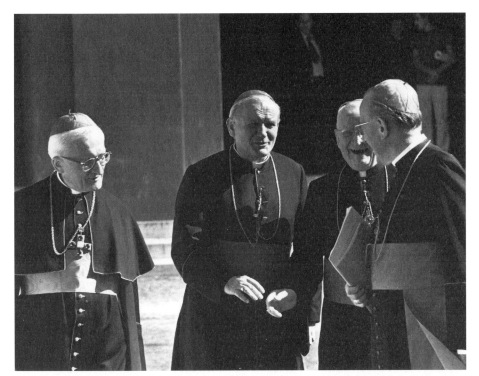

FAR LEFT: *Three years before his election as pope, John Paul II greets Polish miners in Wawel Cathedral, Kracow. His deep concern for Poland's workers led him to give strong support to Solidarity a few years later.*

LEFT: *The new pope shares a joke with some of the cardinals who elected him in St. Peter's Square a few days after his elevation to the papacy.*

BELOW: *John Paul II greets the crowds from the main loggia of St. Peter's Basilica on October 16, 1978, the day of his election. He became the 264th pontiff.*

THE TRAVELING POPE

LEFT: *The pope cradles a Mexican Indian child during his visit to the impoverished village of Cuilapan. John Paul's trip to Mexico in January 1979 was his first foreign tour as pope.*

RIGHT: *Ten years later John Paul was still globe-trotting. Here he waves to a crowd of South Koreans from the steps of his Alitalia papal plane in Seoul.*

John Paul II was installed as pope in St. Peter's Square on October 22, 1978 in front of 250,000 people and millions of television viewers worldwide. From the first few months of his papacy it was clear that, in style at least, the papal mold had been broken. No longer would the bishop of Rome be a silent, distant figure who barely ventured from the Vatican: the new pope was an extremely visible and truly global pastor. Yet the amazing whirlwind of visits which were to become a hallmark of John Paul II were not the result of a carefully planned strategy. They simply multiplied as each tour sparked innumerable requests from other Catholics eager to share in the excitement and spiritual awareness that the pope engendered on his visits.

The first foreign tour was to Latin America in January 1979 in response to a long-standing invitation from its bishops to attend the Episcopal Conference of Latin America (CELAM) in Puebla, Mexico (both Paul VI and John Paul I had been invited but due to their deaths the conference was rescheduled to allow a new pope to attend). The

conference was inevitably overshadowed, however, by the massive outpouring of joy that greeted his arrival. Up to 10 million Mexicans lined the pope's route from Mexico City to Puebla, and it was fitting that his first overseas trip was to a Third World country, where the majority of the world's Catholics now live. But the trip

ABOVE: *John Paul makes an historic return to his homeland.*

RIGHT: *A beautiful floral facade welcomes John Paul to Mexico City in 1979.*

BELOW: *John Paul raises the chalice at his investiture mass.*

was not simply an opportunity for celebration. John Paul had brought a message and it was by no means a straightforward one. In some respects it was not what many Latin Americans wished to hear.

A previous meeting of CELAM in Medellin, Columbia, which was called to implement Vatican II in Latin America, had seen the birth of what became known as Liberation Theology. The prevalence of oppressive authoritarian governments and extreme poverty had naturally turned the minds of many priests toward politics: and as many of their governments were right-wing, these politics took on a distinctly socialist character. There had been a conservative reaction among some clergy to these views, but when the conference met at Puebla most of the bishops sought to reaffirm "the preferential option for the poor" set out at Medellin.

Against this background the pope spoke out strongly against the injustices perpetrated in Latin America and seemed sympathetic toward the fundamental concerns of the poor and their priests, but he warned the clergy that they should not get too involved with politics. "You are not social directors, political leaders, or functionaries of temporal power. . . . Do not forget that temporal leadership can easily become a source of division." He also argued that radical reinterpretations of the

ABOVE: *A Black Madonna and child, similar to the icon in the shrine at Jasna Gora in Czestochowa. Czestochowa is Poland's most important shrine and the Black Madonna is given the credit for holding Swedish invaders at bay in the seventeenth century, thus saving Poland from foreign domination.*

RIGHT: *John Paul (standing in red) celebrates mass in the open before a Polish crowd in his beloved Kracow.*

ABOVE: *The famous Jasna Gora monastery in Czestochowa, Poland. In 1717 the Black Madonna was ceremonially crowned as "Queen of Poland." A title which Poles still use today.*

LEFT: *John Paul visits Auschwitz concentration camp just outside Kracow.*

Gospel which portrayed Christ as a political revolutionary championing the cause of the poor were incorrect and based on "theoretical speculation" rather than "authentic meditation."

This seemingly contradictory message encapsulates John Paul II's thinking on the role of the Church in politics. The Church should sympathize with the poor and oppressed, and speak out on their behalf, but it should not become too politically active nor seek confrontation with governments. Of course the line between criticism and political activity is difficult to draw, and the pope himself was often accused of overstepping it in his own country of Poland, but we can understand the distinction in

terms of his belief in the primacy of faith and religious liberty over politics. For while John Paul II is undoubtedly concerned with injustice and material well-being, for him these are of lesser importance than the ability to practice one's religion freely. Hence, the Church should not take strong political stances against individual governments for this would invite persecution and jeopardize the religious freedom of its people.

John Paul II's profound regard for human dignity and his insistence that no human should be regarded as a tool but cherished in his own right inspires damning critiques of many social and economic conditions, but these are always couched in very general terms

or even buried in opaque religious argument. This approach may be somewhat infuriating to liberal-minded Catholics, but when seen in the context of his 30-year struggle to keep the Church alive in an unsympathetic regime, they at least become understandable.

The visit to Mexico was followed by an emotional return to Poland in June. After an uncomfortable meeting with First Secretary Eduard Gierek, in which John Paul diplomatically spoke of the basic rights of nations to political self-determination, he said mass before a jubilant crowd of over 250,000 in Warsaw. He then flew to the birthplace of Polish Christianity, Gniezo, for mass with an even larger gathering of half a

ABOVE: *John Paul flew directly from Ireland to the U.S.A. Here he shakes hands with President Jimmy Carter on the North Lawn of the White House in October 1979 during a reception in the pope's honor.*

RIGHT: *Jubilant admirers of John Paul wave the distinctive yellow and white flag of the Vatican state during his visit to Ireland in 1979.*

million. He made a thinly-veiled criticism of the Communist government for attempting to keep Christ out of the history of humanity, and the crowd loved it. Czestochowa, home of the Black Madonna of Jasna Gora, was next, and 3.5 million people flocked to the spiritual heart of Poland to see him. John Paul spoke to the conference of Polish bishops there on the need to "normalize" the relations between Church and state and dedicated his papacy to the Black Madonna.

No tour would have been complete without a return to his former diocese of Kracow, and the last few days included visits to his home town of Wadowice (where he was greeted by his former teacher Father Zacher), to Nowa Huta, and most memorably to Auschwitz. In Auschwitz John Paul prayed in the cell of Maximilian Kolbe (the priest who sacrificed himself for

the sake of a married man chosen for execution and who John Paul later beatified) and then presided over mass among the barbed wire fences of the nearby Birkenau concentration camp: an event that everyone present found deeply moving.

A trip to Ireland followed in the fall, and it was obvious that the unhappy history of Ireland and its devotion to Mary struck a chord with the Polish pope. He fiercely condemned the use of violence in the pursuit of political goals at a mass in Dublin's Phoenix Park and visited the Marian shrine at Knock. He had never planned to visit Northern Ireland, but in any case the Rev. Ian Paisley announced that he would organize a general strike if he did and predictably thought that the pope's message gave comfort to the IRA, although it is difficult to see why. At a mass in Drogheda near the border he stated: "Violence is a crime against humanity . . . I pray with you that the moral sense and Christian conviction of Irish men and women may never become obscured and blunted by the lie of violence, that nobody may ever call murder by any other name than murder, that the spiral of violence may never be given the distinction of unavoidable logic or necessary retaliation."

After this successful trip to Ireland, John Paul flew directly to Boston for an American tour that included visits to New York, Chicago, and a meeting with President Carter at the White House. However, as with Mexico, the pastoral element of the visit had developed at a late stage and the original reason for going to the U.S.A. was an invitation to speak at the United Nations.

ABOVE: *John Paul enjoys a traditional New York ticker-tape welcome.*

RIGHT: *John Paul preaches to the American faithful in 1979.*

BELOW: *John Paul with the Greek Orthodox Patriarchy in Istanbul.*

LEFT: *The Greek Orthodox patriarch, Demetrius I embraces Pope John Paul II at Istanbul Airport. The pontiff was beginning a three-day visit which aimed to bring the Roman Catholic and Greek Orthodox churches closer together. The two churches have been divided since a schism in 1054.*

RIGHT: *John Paul made two major foreign tours in 1980. On his trip to Africa he traveled nearly 12,000 miles and visited Zaire, Congo, Kenya, Ghana, Burkina Faso, and the Ivory Coast. Here he is in Nairobi, Kenya blessing a young mother and her children.*

BELOW RIGHT: *Kenyan President Daniel Arap Moi greets John Paul as he arrives at Jomo Kenyatta International Airport in Nairobi.*

The pope was given a welcome which surprised him with its warmth and intensity, but this did not deter him from speaking his mind on issues that made many uncomfortable. John Paul used the visit to expound his criticisms of Western consumerism in its ideological home, just as he had attacked Communism in Poland. He had attacked consumerism in Ireland, but this was merely a warning to the youth of a newly emerging consumer society to avoid "the empty pursuit of mere material possessions." The speech he gave to the United Nations was more fundamental. In his desire to promote the cause of world peace he identified many of the underlying causes of international tension as economic, and his address was a thinly-disguised attack on global capitalism. "The relationship between states and even between entire continents contain within themselves substantial elements that restrict or violate human rights. Such elements are the exploitation of labor and many other abuses that affect the dignity of the human person."

There is little in John Paul's philosophy to comfort the Marxist or the capitalist. Essentially both are materialistic rather than spiritual and hence both fail to recognize that work is only valuable as a human activity and not because it produces material goods. For John Paul human dignity is central. Any economic system which loses sight of this and treats humans as productive tools is inevitably flawed.

The pope's hectic first year in office ended with a low-key visit to Turkey to build some bridges with the Orthodox patriarch, Demetrius I. The rapprochement between the Roman and Eastern churches was of major interest to John Paul, and the complex religious geography and history of the Slavic lands of Eastern Europe and Russia were to be a constant preoccupation. In the West, the ecumenical movement is primarily an attempt to improve relations be-

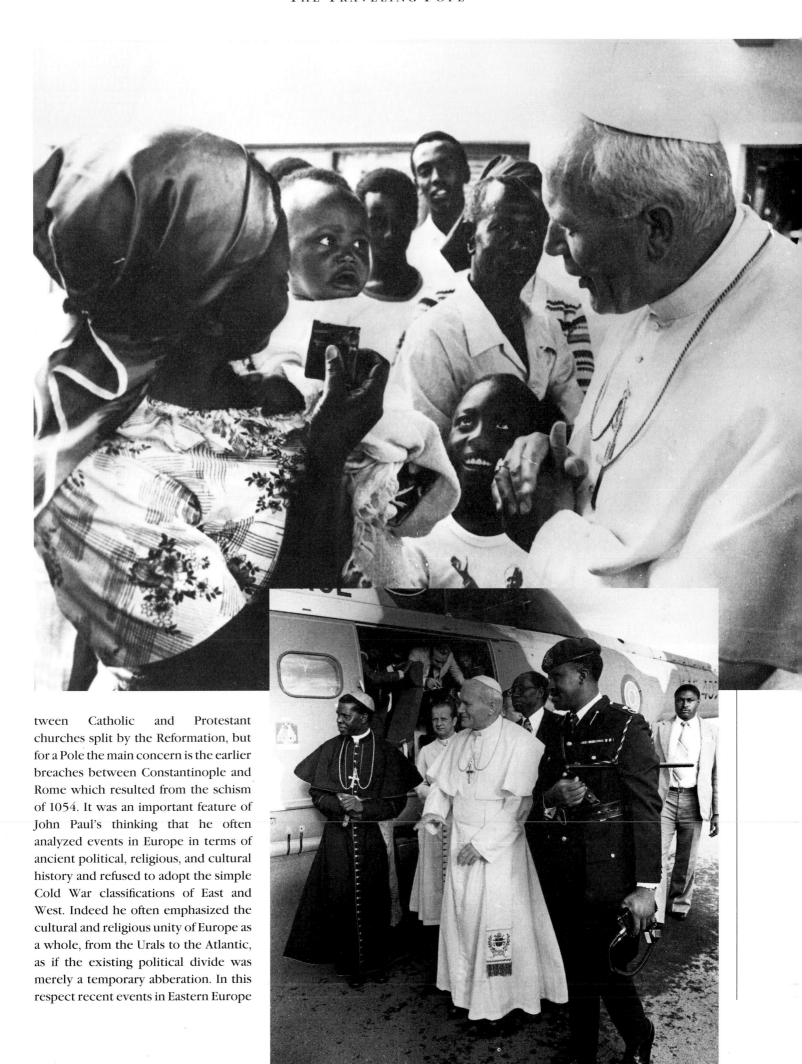

tween Catholic and Protestant churches split by the Reformation, but for a Pole the main concern is the earlier breaches between Constantinople and Rome which resulted from the schism of 1054. It was an important feature of John Paul's thinking that he often analyzed events in Europe in terms of ancient political, religious, and cultural history and refused to adopt the simple Cold War classifications of East and West. Indeed he often emphasized the cultural and religious unity of Europe as a whole, from the Urals to the Atlantic, as if the existing political divide was merely a temporary abberation. In this respect recent events in Eastern Europe have shown his grand historical perspective to be more perceptive than it seemed at the time.

This profoundly European outlook has, however, raised some doubts about his ability to respond sympathetically to the problems of the growing Third World churches. Continuing the pattern of world tours, 1980 saw important visits to Africa and Brazil (as well as shorter trips to West Germany and France) and both these major tours threw up their problems for the pope. The first African tour was especially welcome as the continent has a large and rapidly expanding Catholic population, but the balance between conformity to the traditional Catholic forms and the "Africanization" of ritual and social doctrine was a contentious issue. The problem of a relatively new religion accommodating ancient social and cultural traditions which often diverged from traditional Christian beliefs (particularly about the role of women in the community, marriage, and sexuality) was a pressing concern for the African bishops.

Typically, John Paul trod an ambiguous path which offered something for all but caused concern in progressive African circles. He asserted the universality of the gospel which "is not identified with any culture, and transcends them all." Yet he insisted that a substantial unity be maintained with Rome in respect of rite and liturgy and emphasized the Catholic positions on monogamous marriages and priestly celibacy. Despite the pope's obvious affection for certain aspects of the African attitude to life, it was not thought proper that he be treated to a full Zairian mass with spears, dancing priests, and headdresses. The tour of Zaire, Congo, Kenya, Ghana, Burkina Faso, and the Ivory Coast was nonetheless a joyous occasion for all, not least the pope himself who was often seen tapping his feet to the African music.

Brazil has some of the greatest extremes of wealth and poverty anywhere in the world, and with his usual blend of stern, yet generalized, social criticism, John Paul gave the Brazilian government much food for thought. He toured

TOP FAR LEFT: *The second of John Paul's major 1980 trips was to Brazil. Over one million people attended this mass in Sao Paulo; the pope is consecrating the altar before the ceremony.*

FAR LEFT: *In 1981 John Paul visited Japan and is seen here talking to Emperor Hirohito in the Imperial Palace in Tokyo.*

ABOVE: *When he visited Favela do Vidigal, a hillside slum in Rio de Janeiro, the pope pledged his support for the cause of Brazil's poor.*

LEFT: *Kissing the ground on arrival in a new country became a trademark of John Paul II. The tarmac at Orly Airport near Paris has the honor this time.*

some of the most degraded areas, speaking to slum dwellers, plantation laborers, and lepers. Twenty million saw him in person and were no doubt inspired by his support for workers' rights and social reform, yet he prohibited direct political action on behalf of the clergy to achieve these goals, just as he had done in Mexico. Nevertheless this tour was, if anything, an even greater triumph than Africa and was described by *The Universe* as "the most extraordinary papal journey in history."

The following year saw an ambitious trip to the Far East which took in the Philippines and Japan, where the pope said mass at Hiroshima and Nagasaki and visited victims of the atomic bombs that were dropped there. As ever, John Paul used his ability to make the location reinforce his message. He appealed for world peace and prayed that the horrific power of nuclear weapons never be used again. His time in the Philippines

TOP: *John Paul, moments after being shot in St. Peter's Square.*

ABOVE RIGHT: *A vigil in St. Peter's Square to pray for the pope.*

ABOVE: *The would-be killer of John Paul, Ahmed Ali Agca, meets the pope in his cell at Rome's Rebibbia Jail two years after the assassination attempt.*

RIGHT: *From a balcony in the pope's summer residence at Castel Gandolfo, John Paul gives his first general audience four months after the attempt to take his life.*

once again posed the dilemma of speaking out against poverty, oppression, and corruption in a country that had turned them into a fine art. Ferdinando Marcos, the infamous former president, was treated to a forthright speech on human rights, but John Paul again condemned violence and the class struggle. The basic political message for oppressed and impoverished countries was now firmly established, and it would change little in the next decade and a half.

On May 13, 1981 the busy schedule of tours was brought to an abrupt halt and this unique papacy itself was almost brought to a tragically early end. In St. Peter's Square, while the pope was giving one of his regular general audiences, Ahmed Ali Agca shot John Paul in the chest. The pope collapsed in his jeep and was rushed into the Vatican and then on to hospital for a difficult five-hour operation. Fortunately the 60 year old was a fit man for his age and the operation was successful. He immediately forgave the young Turk who had tried to kill him and began his recuperation. Rumors began to emerge of KGB involvement, but the evidence was sketchy. The Vatican obviously suspected that Ali Agca (a convicted assassin who had already made clear his intention to kill the pope in a Turkish newspaper) was the tool of a Communist plot to prevent the high-profile Slav from using his position to destabilize Poland and the rest of Eastern Europe. However sufficient proof was never obtained.

There were some complications with blood poisoning, but John Paul made a good recovery, no doubt aided by the thousands of heartfelt messages he received wishing him a speedy return to health. The news of the death of his old friend and former superior Cardinal Wyszynski just two weeks after the attack was a further blow, but in October he finally resumed his official duties. Many think that he still bears the mental scars of the attack to this day, and his recent remarks about the spiritual value of suffering, which referred directly to the assassination attempt, would seem to confirm this view. John Paul had had a lucky escape.

SOLIDARITY AND DIVERSITY

BELOW: *John Paul II and Soviet President Mikhail Gorbachev meet at the Vatican on November 18, 1990 nearly a year after their ground-breaking first encounter.*

RIGHT: *During his 1982 visit to the U.K., John Paul gives his blessing to the congregation of Westminster Cathedral.*

As John Paul recovered his strength, events in Poland weighed heavily on his mind. In December 1981 General Jaruzelski, Poland's first secretary and prime minister, had declared martial law as Soviet intervention seemed imminent. Poland had seen sporadic outbreaks of unrest and protest since the mass demonstrations in 1956 (which had led to the death of 50 people), and in 1970-71 and 1976 rises in food prices had caused further strikes and the emergence of a radical workers' movement centered on the Lenin shipyards in Gdansk. During the early 1980s the situation became extremely tense.

Emboldened and inspired by John Paul's visit in 1979, Poles became increasingly critical of the Communist party, which had led Poland into a desperate economic situation. The announcement of price rises on July 1, 1980 was the catalyst for spontaneous strikes all over the country, and when the Gdansk shipyard workers went on strike in August, it was clear to the government that it was not just price rises that were the issue: fundamental political concerns had to be addressed. Choosing to negotiate, the government signed the Gdansk Agreement with the strikers; and so Solidarity, the Commu-

nist block's first "independent, self-managing labor union," was born.

The pope's meeting with Lech Walesa, the leader of Solidarity, in January 1981 was a symbol of the active spiritual, political (and probably financial) support John Paul was providing. The Communists were scathing in their criticism, arguing that John Paul was instigating the "anti-socialist activities of the reactionary clergy in Poland" and

illegitimately interfering in their internal affairs. When the Polish government reneged on part of the Gdansk Agreement concerning working on Saturdays, it was clear that they had no intention of enacting the changes agreed in the accord and so Solidarity planned its first conference for October 1981, effectively becoming a political party as opposed to a simple labor union. Their plans for a day of national

ABOVE: *Lech Walesa, the leader of Solidarity, receives holy communion from his fellow Pole in 1987 during a mass in Gdansk, one of the main centers of Polish opposition to the Communist regime.*

RIGHT: *In the same city of Gdansk, John Paul has a strong message for Poland's youth. He urges them to stand up for their rights and not to remain silent.*

FAR RIGHT: *During the same 1987 tour John Paul kisses the grave of Jerzy Popieluszko, a pro-Solidarity priest who was murdered by the police in 1984.*

protest on December 17 were scotched, however, as martial law was imposed five days earlier. Solidarity's leaders were arrested, its buildings seized, and the movement was declared illegal.

The Vatican issued strong condemnations and an unusually strident John Paul appealed to the international community to address these injustices. Martial law was only lifted in July 1983, and during this period the Polish government was reluctant to allow John Paul to return to his homeland for fear that he might provide a focus for opposition. The economic situation had not been improved during the period of martial

law, however, and the spirit of opposition, partly attributable to the pope, remained. Throughout this period the pope met secretly with Walesa during his trips to Poland and was a constant source of inspiration and national pride. It would be reasonable to argue that John Paul was a major factor in the freedoms gained by Poland and her neighbors in 1989.

The changing conditions which allowed Solidarity to prevail also led to the second important papal intervention in the Communist bloc, for *glasnost* caused a softening of Moscow's attitude to the Church as well as a weak-

FAR LEFT: *The historic first meeting between John Paul and Mikhail Gorbachev on December 1, 1989. The pope listened pensively to Gorbachev's speech, and real progress was rapidly made.*

ABOVE: *After her visit to the Vatican in 1980, John Paul returns the compliment and visits Queen Elizabeth II at Buckingham Palace in May 1982.*

FAR RIGHT: *A woman in a wheelchair kisses the pope's hand during his walkabout in Rosewell, Scotland in June 1982.*

BELOW: *John Paul seems delighted to be giving holy communion to some Scottish youngsters on another stop in his tour of Britain. This mass was at Bellahouston Park in Glasgow.*

ening of the Communists' grip on power. Until Gorbachev was firmly established, relations between the Soviets and the Vatican had been uneasy (although there was some contact, such as the pope's meetings with Foreign Minister Gromyko in 1979 and 1985). But after some encouraging signals from Gorbachev in 1987, John Paul was able to send 10 cardinals to the Russian Orthodox church's millennium celebrations in 1988, and on December 1, 1989 the two greatest living Slavs met when Gorbachev paid an official visit to the Vatican. The two men seemed to like each other and they announced that diplomatic relations between Moscow and the Holy See were to be resumed.

It was an historic moment. The leader of the atheistic Communist world and the world's most important spiritual leader had agreed to work together both for world peace, and crucially for the pope, religious freedom in the Soviet Union. The first steps toward the re-establishment of the Ukrainian Catholic church

were taken when the Soviets immediately announced its eligibility for legal status, and in the following October they finally passed the law on the freedom of worship that Gorbachev had promised. There are still many difficulties to be overcome between the Ukrainian Catholics and the state-sponsored Orthodox church (primarily over church buildings which were confiscated by the state on behalf of the Orthodox church after World War II, when Ukrainian Catholicism was brutally suppressed), and to some extent these new freedoms have worsened relations between Rome and the Orthodox churches. However, the religious freedom gained for these particularly devout Catholics must be regarded as one of John Paul's triumphs. Of course, the Ukrainians themselves had played a vital role, as resurgent Ukrainian nationalism had combined with demands for religious recognition. But, as in the case of Poland, the spiritual support and diplomacy of the pope should not be underestimated.

By this stage Eastern Europe had already taken its first decisive steps to freedom. Gorbachev's policy of *glasnost* had set in motion trends toward "open" government, and by August 1989, after a period of limited power-sharing, Solidarity's Tadeusz Mazowiecki became the first non-Communist prime minister in Eastern Europe. Only three weeks earlier the Berlin Wall had come down, Czechoslovakia's Communist government had just resigned, and Hungary was heading for its first free elections. It would not be long before the Soviet Union itself felt the full impact of the forces unleashed by Gorbachev, and in the post-Cold War era the pope's mission to promote world peace and religious freedom must meet new and complex challenges.

John Paul would readily acknowledge that as a global spiritual leader he had many other pressing concerns during the 1980s apart from his Euro-

pean political and religious diplomacy. Rapid transformations in the geographical make-up of the church had brought into question its Eurocentric outlook and led to calls for greater diversity or "enculturization" within the Church. Massive population increases and the spread of AIDS had provoked severe criticism of the Church's teaching on contraception; the lowly position of women within Catholicism was unacceptable to many; and there was pressure within the Church to press ahead more quickly with ecumenical efforts to bridge the gaps with other faiths. The triumphs of foreign tours and diplomacy would count for little if he failed to address the issues which were central to the health, and indeed survival, of the Catholic church.

To understand how John Paul tackled these concerns we should look briefly at the style of his papacy and his concept of papal authority. The principle of

ABOVE: *In 1986, John Paul visited Chief Rabbi Elio Taoff in his Rome synagogue. This was the first ever visit to a Jewish house of worship by a head of the Roman Catholic church.*

FAR LEFT: *Cardinal Malula, archbishop of Kinshasa in Zaire, looks slightly suspicious as his flock get excited about John Paul in August 1985. Perhaps he realizes the pope will be a hard act to follow when he flies back to Rome.*

collegiality (the idea that the bishops should, collectively, have a major part in making important doctrinal decisions) was one of the main thrusts of Vatican II and was enthusiastically advocated by John Paul before and after his election. However, his papacy immediately took on a more authoritarian style and the much-vaunted synods of bishops were allowed little real power when it came to fundamental doctrinal decision-making.

The Vatican documents that eventually emerged from these synods often bore little relation to the majority views expressed, and on occasion they could have been produced without the synod meeting at all. National episcopates with strong liberal tendencies, such as the American and Dutch, were subjected to close papal scrutiny and appointments of bishops and cardinals were often overt attempts to promote clergy with similar views to the pope

ABOVE: *John Paul bears little resemblance to a eucalyptus tree, but the Koala bear seems happy enough with the pontiff's presence in Brisbane, Australia in 1986.*

RIGHT: *After performing an ancient spiritual dance, these aboriginal men kiss the pope's hand in Blatherskite Park near Alice Springs on the same Australian tour.*

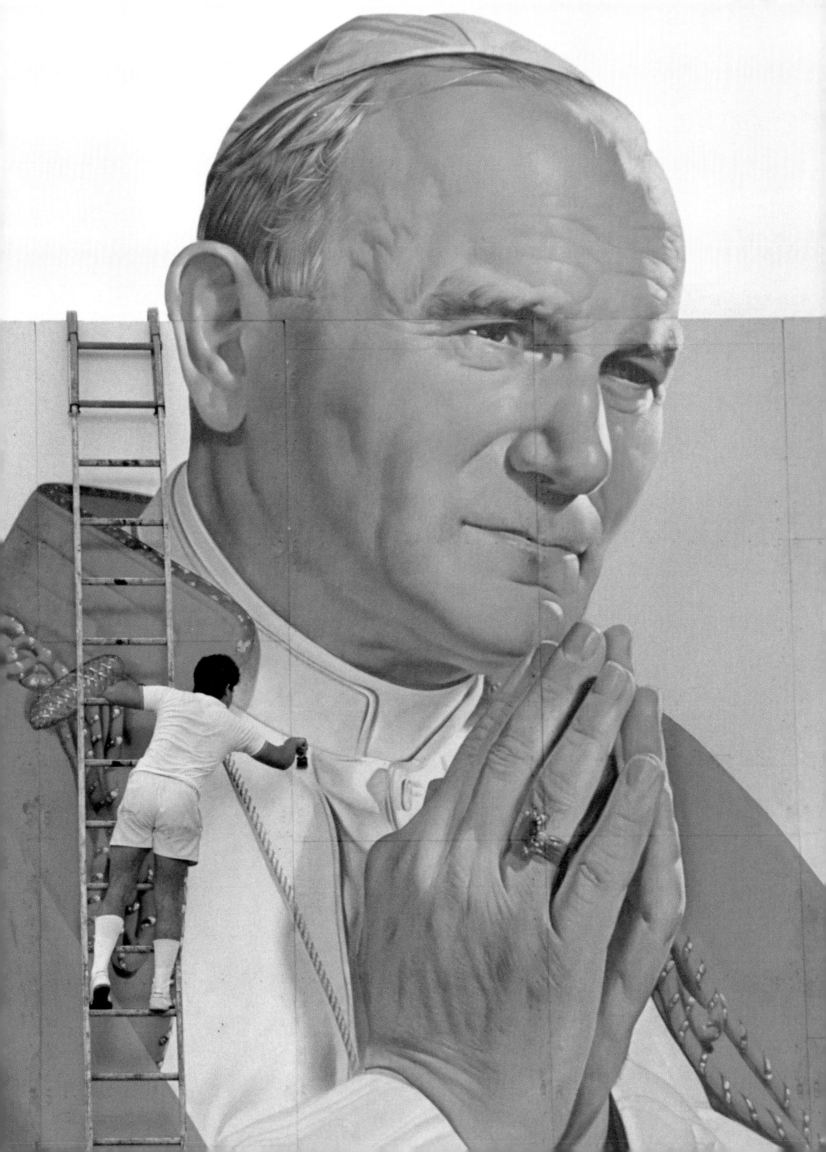

Divergences from accepted modes of theological speculation were also dealt with more strictly than in the immediate past. Of course any organized church must have some limitations on what its members are allowed to teach in its name or else it would never maintain its identity and purpose, but many thought that John Paul's use of Cardinal Ratzinger and the Congregation for the Doctrine of Faith went too far. Even the fiercely independent Jesuits became the objects of intense papal scrutiny after their alleged involvement with Marxist politics in Latin America.

How far John Paul's actions were a deliberate attempt to increase the pontiff's power as opposed to the inevitable outcome of his traditional views and background is debatable. But in his attempt to unify and strengthen the church he has exhibited authoritarian tendencies which have dismayed many inside and outside the Catholic faith. As many clergy and laity wrestle with increasingly complex global problems, the pope seems unwilling to rethink doctrine in the light of new conditions. An important example of this tendency is John Paul's attempts, or lack of them, to make the African church more appealing to its members.

After his first visit, John Paul undertook further trips to Africa in 1982, 1985, 1988, 1989, 1990 (twice), 1992, and 1993. He seemed genuinely to enjoy the color, spirit, and life of these joyful occasions and it was often evident that he admonished moral failings less harshly in Africa than elsewhere, but there are many pressing issues for the pope to address in this ethnically and religiously diverse continent. One of the most pressing is the "collision course" some predict between Islam and Christianity.

Islam is the world's fastest growing religion and is about to overtake Catholicism as the largest individual religious group. By the end of the century it is predicted that 42 percent of Africa's population will be Christian and 48 percent Muslim. In some African states, such as Sudan, Islam is already the state religion, and many African Muslims, such as those in Nigeria, are pressing for

their countries to impose Islam as a state religion. In 1985 the pope had to cancel a visit to predominantly Muslim Senegal, as Muslim activists threatened to lie down on the runway to stop him from landing.

John Paul has tried to build bridges with Islam. In their shared monotheism he sees a potential ally in an increasingly faithless world, and his reception in Morocco by the people, and King Hassan, in 1985 was warm and positive.

ABOVE: *The last few yards of the famous pilgrimage route to Santiago de Compostela in Spain is successfully negotiated by John Paul with a pilgrim cape and staff in August 1989.*

FAR LEFT: *This huge billboard of John Paul was erected on Biscayne Boulevard to welcome him to Miami, the first port of call on his nine-city U.S. tour of 1987.*

TOP: *Judging by the flags you might think John Paul was in Cuba. He is actually opening his 1987 U.S. tour in Miami. An estimated 200,000 turned up for this mass.*

ABOVE: **Hundreds of South Korean girls greet the pontiff with national and Vatican flags as he lands at Seoul Airport in 1989.**

FAR RIGHT: *From Korea John Paul headed to Indonesia. Here he blesses dancers in traditional costumes on his arrival in Yogyakarta for mass.*

Christian community are imposed on all of Sudan's citizens.

Another problem he faces is the proliferation of other Christian sects and churches in Africa. Evangelization by established Protestant churches is proving more effective than Catholic evangelization, and many smaller sects with distinctly dubious "gospels of prosperity" have made inroads in West Africa as well as (more predictably) among the affluent whites of South Africa. At the root of these problems lies the pope's attitude to the acceptance of African culture by the local churches and his authority over them.

The pope has been criticized for his reluctance to take "enculturization" further, but this is not a simple problem. Indigenous spiritual and cultural traditions may be valuable, but just how far can traditional beliefs about polygamy and animism be incorporated without fundamentally contradicting the teaching of the Gospel? Can the worship of ancestral spirits be simply transformed into appeals to the saints? Furthermore, if the Church is to be truly "Catholic" (i.e. universal), surely a significant degree of doctrinal and liturgical uniformity must be maintained?

As John Paul stated in Cameroon in 1985, "a rupture between the Gospel and culture would be a tragedy," but for the pope it is culture which must change if in conflict with the Gospel. On his tour of Mozambique in 1988, he explicitly stated that liturgy in the African church must "respect with loving and total fidelity the texts and rites which the legitimate authority has decided to exclude from the creativity of individuals and groups." John Paul was given much food for thought on these issues when he presided over the first synod of African bishops in April and May of 1994 at the Vatican. The Vatican document that emerges from this synod will, as has become customary, no doubt bear closer resemblance to John Paul's view of "Africanization" than the majority view in the synod. However, perhaps because of this, it will take on even greater importance as a statement of intent by the Church for the future of the continent.

However, the growth of fundamentalism and a sense of Islamic community has not made relations easy. John Paul caused controversy in Sudan when he quite reasonably argued that if a state adopts an official religion "it cannot claim to impose that religion on its people or restrict the religious freedom of other citizens." But the problem is not simply one of religious toleration. Human rights groups have noted an increasingly hostile environment for Christians in many African countries (such as Egypt), and in Sudan, for example, civil and criminal codes now adhere to Islamic law and many punishments that are seen as barbaric by the

JOHN PAUL AND HUMAN LIFE

BELOW: *Emmett White, a Pima Native American medicine man, presents John Paul with an American eagle feather during his stopover at Phoenix, Arizona on the 1987 tour.*

RIGHT: *Demonstrating his amazing gift for languages, John Paul gave part of his 1990 Easter Sunday message in Lithuanian and called for peace in the republic.*

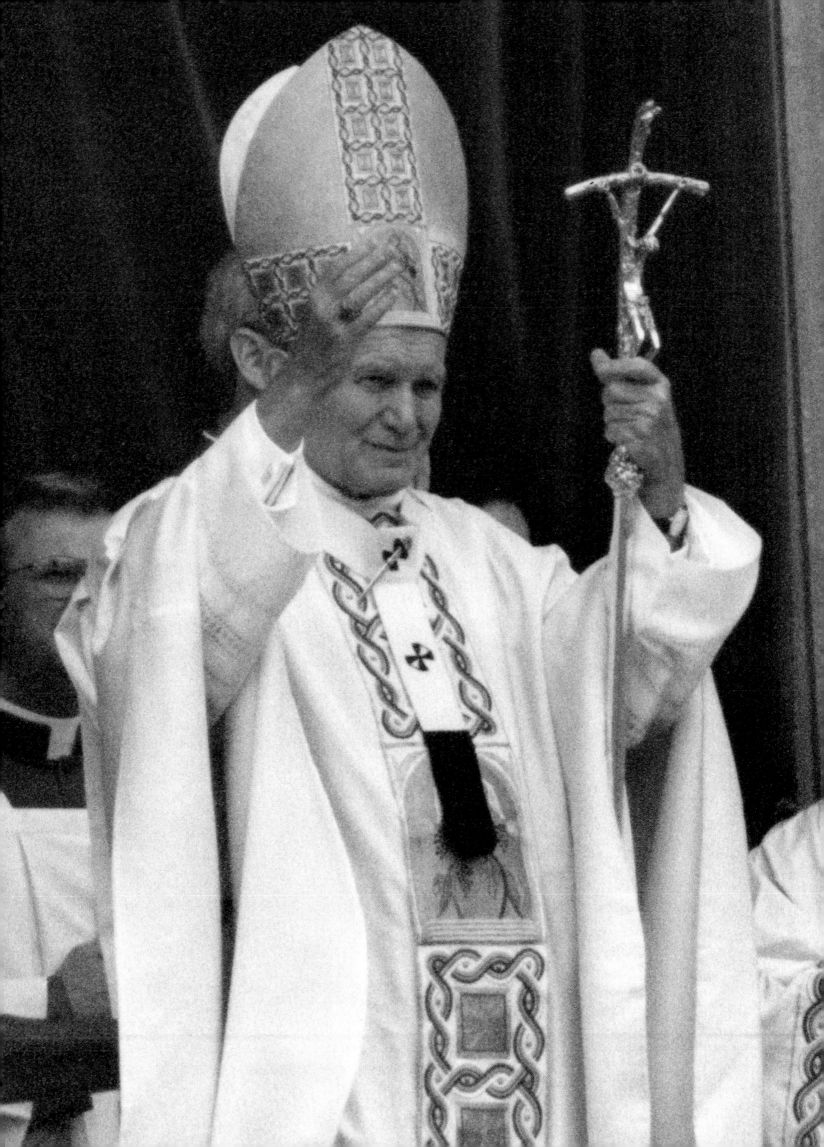

No examination of the pope's life and beliefs would be complete without looking at his views on contraception, the family, and the role of women. It is the first of these issues that is perhaps the most pressing, for the world is faced with an unprecedented population crisis. A global population of six billion is estimated for the end of the century (the figure was only half this as recently as the late 1950s), and as the Catholic church has almost one billion members worldwide, many of them in the areas of most rapid growth such as Africa and Latin America, the Church's opposition to family planning and artificial birth control has obvious significance. Furthermore, the defense of its position has come to be regarded as a personal crusade of John Paul.

ABOVE: *An old Lithuanian woman waits patiently for her hero.*

RIGHT: *John Paul blesses thousands during a mass in Prahia, Cape Verde.*

ABOVE: *Leading a candle-lit Good Friday procession through the Colosseum in Rome in 1990, John Paul carries a large wooden cross in remembrance of Christ's crucifixion.*

RIGHT: *In 1993, John Paul made another U.S. tour. This mass is taking place in front of half a million people at Cherry Creek State Park in Colorado.*

John Paul's firm condemnation of contraception is basically in line with Paul VI's as outlined in his encyclical *Humanae Vitae.* An important difference, however, is that Paul VI never defined his rejection of artificial birth control as part of the infallible teaching of Catholicism. John Paul has raised the stakes rather than leave the door open for a future reappraisal: he has defined contraception as a "denial of God." For the pope, to use contraception is to put yourself in the place of God by choosing which humans come into existence and which do not, and in 1987 John Paul stated that "what is taught by the Church on contraception is not a matter that can be discussed freely by theologians." It is difficult to see any change in his position on this issue.

John Paul is well conversant with the problem of demographic growth, yet he is unwavering in his thinking. He criticized artificial birth control in every one of the African countries he visited during his first 1990 tour, and although he showed a deep concern for the fight against AIDS, he ruled out the use of condoms to combat the disease. However, the pope's views have not deterred Catholics in Western countries from agonizing over the use of contraceptives and using their own consciences in this matter. It is clear that the majority of them have rejected natural birth control in favor of more reliable artificial methods, and the divergence between doctrine and practice has been deeply corrosive on Church authority.

Of course criticism from outside the Church is even more vociferous. Most experts agree that natural methods of birth control are particularly unsuitable for the uneducated and poor Third World couples which are at the heart of the problem, and the omission of the issue of population control from the agenda of the "Earth Summit" at Rio de Janeiro in 1992 (largely because of Catholic opposition) caused dismay in many circles. The Anglican archbishop of Canterbury, Dr. George Carey, was among the many who voiced his disappointment. John Paul's increasing isolation on this issue from both the Western nations, and most of the Third World, forced the Vatican into an uneasy alliance with Islamic fundamentalism during the Cairo population conference in September 1994.

Needless to say, abortion is abhorred by the pope and the Church as a whole, but abortion as a means of birth control has become very common in many Catholic countries such as Brazil. Ironically it is also widespread in Poland and the other ex-Communist countries of Eastern Europe, where over 10 million legal abortions are performed each year, despite the automatic excommunication of anyone involved with the operation. But even the obvious correlation between restricted access to contraceptives and high abortion rates has not caused the Vatican to soften its line on artificial birth control.

These views are, in a sense, simply a part of the pope's beliefs about the function and role of families. The synod on the family in 1980 produced some radical suggestions on divorce, remarriage, respect for the cultural diversity of family life, and contraception, but the ensuing papal summary *Familiaris Consortio* simply re-established the traditional teaching. In his opening address to the 1983 Pontifical Council for the Family, John Paul outlined the essentials: there must be a direct link between conjugal love and procreation; the family must accept primary responsibility for the education of its children; and the state must respect the rights and function of the family as a unit. The preservation of "family values" continues to be a primary concern of John Paul's, and in 1994, the International Year of the Family, he wrote to heads of state all over the world to warn of the dangers posed to family life in the modern world.

The role of women, both in the Church and in society as a whole, is another area of controversy. John Paul has an obvious and deep respect for women

FAR LEFT: *During the pope's three-day visit to Chad in 1990, he said mass in La Concorde stadium in Ndjamena. This Chadian woman is wearing a traditional "boubou" with an image of John Paul printed on the back.*

LEFT: *Two beautiful children in Lithuanian national dress receive the pope's attentions in Vilnius in September 1993.*

BELOW: *In February 1993 John Paul set off for yet another African tour. The western Ugandan town of Kasese was the setting for a mass and John Paul blesses a struggling child beforehand.*

ABOVE: *John Paul must have quite a collection of souvenirs from all his trips abroad. After a private audience with Japan's Prime Minister Toshiki Kaifu (left) in 1990 he is given a Japanese vase.*

LEFT: *A young Mexican woman receives an unexpected blessing after she broke through the security cordon at the Los Pinos presidential residence. Mexican President Carlos Salinas doesn't seem too concerned at the lapse in security either.*

RIGHT: *John Paul in familiar pose in the window of his Vatican apartment on January 13, 1991. He is leading prayers for peace in the Gulf.*

RIGHT: *On the last full day of his tour to Brazil in 1991, the pope bids farewell to a large crowd of cheering children and adults near the ornate basilica in Salvador.*

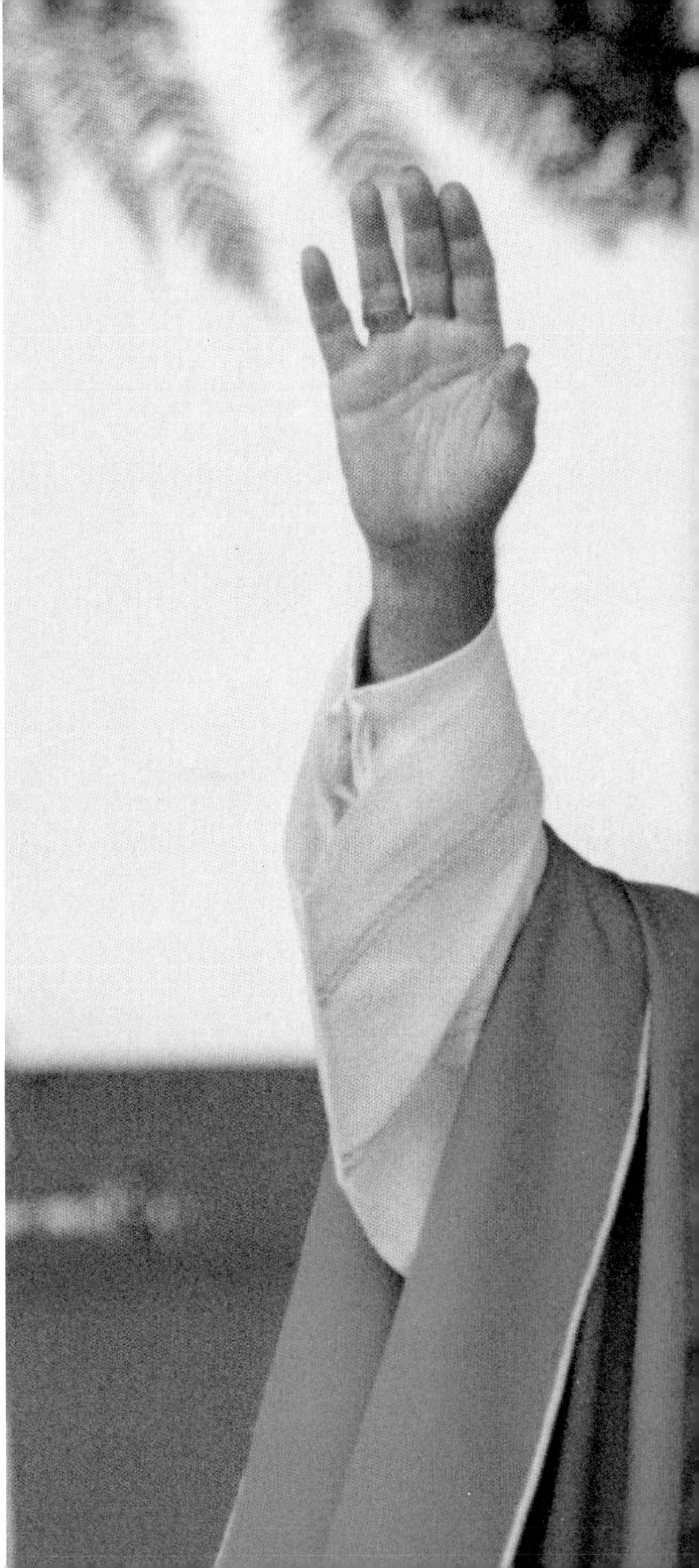

but also has a very traditional view of their role. This is partly based on his devotion to Mary, and in *Redemptoris Mater* he explicitly points to Mary as a feminine role model. "Women, by looking to Mary, find in her the secret of living their own femininity with dignity and of achieving their own true advancement. . . . the self-offering totality of love; the strength that is capable of bearing the greatest sorrows, limitless fidelity and tireless devotion to work; the ability to combine penetrating intuition with words of support and encouragement."

This blueprint for women's spiritual advancement emphasizes supportive and nurturing roles which are viewed with some suspicion in the West, and many feel that women are not valued highly enough by the male-dominated Church. They are certainly not treated as absolute equals, and while John Paul is sympathetic to the increasing demands being placed on women who choose to work and raise a family, it is clear that he values their efforts in the home more highly than those in the workplace. In *Crossing the Threshold of Hope*, published in October 1994, John Paul seems to blame feminism for the predicament of many women. "Woman has become, before all else, an object of pleasure. A certain contemporary feminism finds its roots in the absence of a true respect for women."

At the 1987 synod on the role of the

ABOVE: *John Paul celebrates mass in the former killing fields of an Angolan execution camp in 1992. There was peace in Angola for the first time after three decades of war.*

FAR LEFT: *President Bill Clinton chats with the pope in Denver.*

LEFT: *John Paul leaving the Gemelli hospital in Rome after being treated for a fractured shoulder.*

FOLLOWING PAGES: *John Paul visits the bizarre "Hill of Crosses" in Siauliai, Lithuania.*

laity, the bishops proposed a number of measures to increase the role of women in the running of the Church, yet most of these were withdrawn by the Vatican before the presentation of the final propositions to the pope. In September 1988 John Paul published *Mulieris Dignitatem* (On the Dignity of Women), in which he linked male domination to original sin rather than an unchangeable natural relationship. But he also warned women not to acquire male characteristics in overcoming this domination and reiterated his opposition to the ordination of women.

The worrying decline in numbers of priests, which led to a synod devoted to the problem in 1990, has not altered John Paul's views, despite a halving of the number of priests in some Western countries since Vatican II. John Paul opposes the ordination of women on the grounds that Christ chose only men as his apostles, and he adheres to the traditional view that priests, like Christ, must give themselves completely to the Church and hence be celibate. Thus there is little prospect of this shortage being alleviated by either the admission of women or married men to the priesthood.

In May 1994, the issue of female ordination was decided beyond doubt, for this papacy at least, when John Paul issued his apostolic letter "On reserving priestly ordination to men alone." He declared that the Church had no authority whatsoever to confer priestly

ABOVE: *John Paul has some fun with Native Americans after a mass at Cherry Creek State Park in Colorado. Over 500,000 people attended the mass in August 1993.*

ABOVE RIGHT: *The bullet-proof popemobile parades along the main street in Vilnius, the capital of the newly independent Lithuania.*

RIGHT: *Shortly after South African President F. W. de Klerk was jointly awarded the 1993 Nobel peace prize with Nelson Mandela, he had a Vatican audience with John Paul II.*

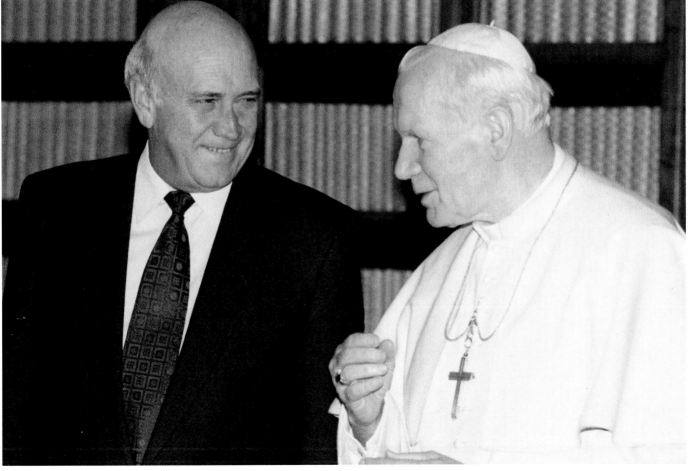

LEFT: *Beneath a glorious blue sky, a magnificent Vatican flag, and a blazing gold canopy, John Paul preaches to Brazil.*

ABOVE: *On September 27, 1992, the pope makes his first appearance after an operation to remove a tumor from his intestines.*

ordination on women and that this judgment was to be definitively held by all the Church's faithful. As well as the offense caused to many women and liberal Catholics, statements such as this have caused difficulties for the ecumenical process with the Protestant churches, particularly the Anglican church which has begun to ordain women.

Undoubtedly John Paul has been a controversial pope, and his traditional outlook has upset many, but he rightly points out that the truth is not always decided by majority opinion. Furthermore, these controversies are, in a sense, peripheral to his essential message. His support for the poor and the ordinary worker, his insistence on the dignity of man as the ultimate goal of any economic or political system, and his criticism of exploitative capitalism with its uneven distribution of resources are all crucial to an understanding of the modern human condition. The pope is also a tireless campaigner for peace in an extremely violent world.

The energy and authority of John Paul have re-established the Vatican as an important player in world affairs and provided humanity with a moral champion at a time when it is crying out for guidance. With well over 50 foreign tours all over the world he has brought the word of God to more people than any other pope in history and taken it to every corner of the globe. And if he has caused divisions within the Church, he has undoubtedly had a great positive influence on the course of world history in the last two decades of the twentieth century.

Until 1992 the pope maintained a phenomenal workload. Since then John Paul has been beset with health problems. In July 1992 the pope entered the Gemelli hospital in Rome for the removal from his colon of a nonmalignant tumor "as large as an orange." The following year, on November 11, the pope slipped walking down steps to greet a UN delegation. He fractured and dislocated his right shoulder, which had to be placed in a cast for a month. Only a few months later, on April 28, 1994, John Paul fell as he was getting out of his shower and broke his right thigh bone.

It was a bad break and required steel pins to help it heal.

One of his senior doctors, Professor Manni, has recently described the pope as "psychologically unwell" and advised him to cut down on his workload. Many who are close to the pope have seen an alarming decline in his health and vigor over the last few years. The endless tours and hectic schedule must have taken their toll on his strength, and some have said that he has never fully recovered psychologically from the assassination attempt in 1981. All this suggests that the final years of John Paul's papacy will see him try to consolidate both his teachings and his papal authority rather than energetically tackle new problems or rethink established doctrine.

It is unlikely that John Paul would consider retirement, but as much of his authority is derived from his sheer energy and force of will, this decline has significant implications for his leadership of the Church. Nevertheless, John Paul has made it clear that he is determined to lead the Church into the third millennium, and despite his recent health problems he has always been a remarkably determined man. We should not be too surprised if he succeeds.

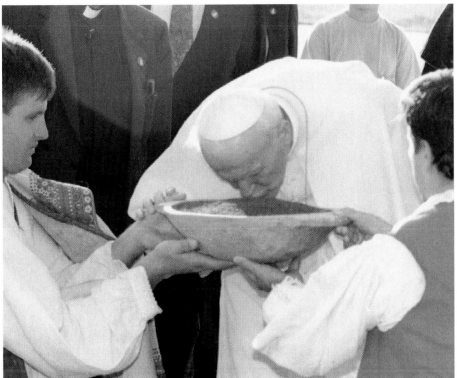

ABOVE: *Representatives of the Archdiocese of Denver are greeted by John Paul, who has joined them for a "Celebration of the Word" on his 1993 U.S. tour.*

FAR LEFT: *An elated Katie Connelly, 17, is embraced by the pope before he boards a helicopter for a trip to Denver.*

LEFT: *Pope John Paul kisses a bowl containing soil instead of kissing the ground upon his arrival at Zagreb Airport in 1994.*

FOLLOWING PAGES: *John Paul tries on a traditional Filipino straw hat and waves to well-wishers in Manila during his 11-day Asian tour, January 1995.*

INDEX

Acknowledgments
The publisher would like to thank Mike Rose for designing this book, Caroline Earle for editing it, Suzanne O'Farrell and Rita Longabucco for the picture research, Nicki Giles for production, and Ron Watson for compiling the index. The following individuals and agencies provided photographic material:
The Bettmann Archive, New York: page 32(top).
Hulton Deutsch Collection Ltd, London: pages 9(top), 14(both), 18(bottom), 20(bottom), 26(top), 22, 35(both), 36(bottom), 37(bottom), 41, 45, 74.
Hulton/Reuters, London: page 63(bottom).
Life File, London: Graham Buchan: page 28(bottom); **Emma Lee:** pages 7, 11, 29(right).
Mirror Syndication International Ltd, London: pages 2-3, 15, 17, 19, 21(bottom), 26(top), 31, 46, 47.
The Polish Press Agency, Warsaw: pages 6(right), 9(bottom right), 10, 12(both), 13, 16(top), 20(top), 28(top).
Reuters/Bettmann, New York: pages 25, 40, 42(top), 43, 44, 48, 49, 50(left), 51, 53, 54(center), 55, 57, 58(left), 58-59, 60, 61, 62, 63(top), 64-65(all 3), 66-67, 68, 69(both), 70-71, 72, 73(both), 75, 76, 77(both), 78, 79.
UPI/Bettmann, New York: pages 1, 4-5, 6(left), 8, 9(bottom left), 16(bottom), 18(top), 23(both), 24, 26(bottom), 27, 29(left), 30, 32(bottom), 33, 34, 36(top), 37(top), 38(both), 39(both), 42(bottom), 52, 54(top), 56.